Last One Home
Is a Green Pig

by EDITH THACHER HURD

Pictures by CLEMENT HURD

An I CAN READ Book

9508

HARPER & ROW, PUBLISHERS
NEW YORK, EVANSTON, AND LONDON

This story is a development and enlargement
of an idea used in a book entitled THE RACE.

Library of Congress catalog card number: 59-8972

Standard Book Number 06-022715-X (Trade Edition)
Standard Book Number 06-022716-8 (Harpercrest Edition)

One day a Duck met a Monkey.

"I will race you home,"

said the Duck to his friend.

"Good," said the Monkey.

"I like to run.

Last one home is a green pig."

"Oh, yes," said the Duck.

"Last one home is a green pig."

The Monkey said,

"One, two.

Get set, go."

Away they went.

The Monkey ran fast.

He ran past the Duck.

Who will be a green pig?

The Duck met

a girl on a bicycle.

"Did you see a Monkey run by?"

he said.

"Yes," said the girl.

"Can you go as fast as that?"

said the Duck.

"Oh, yes," said the girl.

"Then take me with you,"

said the Duck.

"This is a race and I want to win."

Up the hill went the Duck.

Down the hill went the Monkey.

But the girl on the bicycle

was too fast for the Monkey.

"Green pig! Green pig!"

said the Duck.

"The race is not over yet,"

said the Monkey.

"If you play a trick like that,

I will play a trick too."

And he did.

The Monkey met a horse.

"Horse," he said,

"did you see a Duck

who sat like a hat

on the top

of the head

of a girl

on a bicycle?"

"Yes," said the horse.

"Can you go as fast as that?"

"Oh, yes," said the horse.

"Then take me with you,"

said the Monkey.

"This is a race and I want to win."

Up the hill went the horse
with the Monkey.

Down the hill went the bicycle.

with the girl and the Duck.

17

"Look at me.

Look at me," said the Monkey.

"Look at what I can do.

No hands."

"Look at me.

Look at me," said the Duck.

"Look at what I can do.

One foot."

Then the Duck gave too big a hop

on the top

of the head

of the girl

on the bicycle.

And he fell off.

Away went the Monkey on the horse.

Then the Duck met a man

with a dump truck.

"Did you see a Monkey on a horse?"

said the Duck.

"Yes," said the man.

"Can your truck go as fast as that?"

"Oh, yes," said the man.

"I can go as fast as a horse."

"Then take me with you,"

said the Duck.

"This is a race and I want to win."

So the Duck got on the truck.

And away he went.

He went so fast

that he went past the Monkey.

"Green pig! Green pig!"

said the Duck.

"This race is not over yet,"

said the Monkey.

Then bang!

Down went the back of the truck.

Out went the Duck.

There he sat

with a bed on his head

and a thing on his wing

and he could not get up.

"Now who is first?

And who is last?

And who will be the green pig?"

said the Monkey.

Then the Duck jumped up.

And he ran for a bus.

"Oh, will you please

take me with you?"

he said to the driver.

"This is a race and I want to win."

"No ducks in my bus,"

said the driver.

"Then I will ride on top," said the Duck.

Away they went after the Monkey.

"Well," said the horse.

"I am glad that Duck went

down in the dump. Now I

will not have to run so fast."

"Yes," said the Monkey.

"Now I will be first.

And he will be last.

That Duck will look funny

when he is a green pig."

Just then something went past.

It went so fast that the horse

did not see what it was.

"Oh," said the horse.

"What was that?"

"That was the Duck.

He was on the top of a bus,"

said the Monkey.

"Can you run as fast as that?"

"No," said the horse. "Get a taxi."

So the Monkey jumped up

on the top of a taxi.

And away he went.

The taxi went so fast

that it went past the bus.

So the Duck jumped

onto the back of the taxi.

And he gave a nip to the tip

of the tail of the Monkey.

"Oh, oh! Let go! Let go!"

said the Monkey.

But the Duck did not let go.

SO—

Off went the Monkey!

Off went the Duck!

Away went the taxi.

"Oh, oh,

what will I do?"

said the Monkey.

"I know what I will do,"

said the Duck.

"I will swim.

Can you swim?"

"Oh, no," said the Monkey.

"I do not know how to swim.

But I can do this.

Can you?

Look at me.

Look at me.

No hands."

But just then—

Off went the Monkey.

Down, down, down.

"Oh," said the Monkey.

"What do I see?

Is it a boat?

Is it a fish?

What do I see?"

The Monkey did not know if it was

a boat or a fish.

But he hung on

and away he went.

Up, up, up.

"And where is the little Duck now?"
he said.

Then the Duck saw a man and a jeep.

"Help me. Help me,"

said the Duck.

"This is a race and I want to win."

"Well, hop in," said the man.

"Thank you," said the Duck.

"I will sit in the back

on the top of your cow."

What can the Monkey do now?

"Oh, dear," he said.

"There goes the Duck.

Now he will win.

I do not see anything

that can help me.

But what do I hear?"

He heard a fire engine.

The Monkey ran as fast as he could.

Two firemen held out their hands.

"Jump. Jump," they said.

So the Monkey jumped.

"Do you see that Duck
on top of that cow
in the back of that jeep?"
said the Monkey.

"Yes," said the firemen.

"Well," said the Monkey,
"we are having a race
and I want to win."

"That is easy," said the firemen.

"A fire engine can go much faster
than a jeep."

"But where is the fire?"
said the Monkey.

"Here it is," said the firemen.

"All off. All off.

We have to shoot water at the fire."

They all got off

and shot water at the fire.

And the Duck went past.

"Too bad for you!" he said.

"This jeep will take me

all the way home.

I will win and you will be a green pig."

"Oh, oh! What is this?" said the Duck.

Pop-pop-pop-pop.

Pop-pop-pop.

A tire on the jeep went

POP!

Away ran the Monkey.

Then the Monkey saw a train.

It was going very fast.

So he gave a big jump.

"This is faster than a jeep,"
said the Monkey.
"And faster than a fire engine,
and faster than a taxi,
and faster than a dump truck,
and faster than a bus,
and faster than a horse,
and faster than a bicycle.
The Duck cannot find anything
as fast as this."

"Oh," said the Duck.

"Is that so?"

"What will I do now?"

said the Monkey.

"I can run. I can jump.

But I cannot fly."

Just then a plane came along.

"Take me with you. Take me with you,"

said the Monkey.

"This is a race and I want to win."

So the airplane flew down.

"Look at me. Look at me,"

said the Monkey.

He flew past the Duck.

"Look how high I can fly."

"So what?" said the Duck.

"You can fly high,

but can you fly low?"

"No," said the Monkey,

"I cannot fly low.

But it is more fun to fly high."

59

"Yes," said the Duck,

"but there is your house down there.

And there is my house.

So I will fly home.

And you will be the green pig."

So the Duck flew down, down, down.

"Oh, dear," said the Monkey.

"I do not want to be a green pig."

And he wasn't.

Because he got home first.

"Oh, dear," said the Duck.

"Do I look like a little green pig?"

"Oh, no," said the Monkey.

"You look like a nice little Duck to me."

"But of course I DID win,"

said the Monkey.

"Yes," said the Duck. "You did.

But not by much.

Let's have another race tomorrow."

9508

E
H

Hurd, Edith Thacher

Last one home is a
green pig

DATE			